MY SECOND HOME

MY SECOND HOME

Sylvia Plath In Paris, 1956

DAVE HASLAM

First published in the UK in 2020 by Cōnfingō Publishing

249 Burton Road, Didsbury, Manchester, M20 2WA
www.confingopublishing.uk

Art Direction & Typesetting by Zoë McLean, zoe@confingopublishing.uk

Printed by TJ Books Limited

A CIP catalogue record for this book is available from the British Library

ISBN 978-0-9955966-7-2

4 6 8 10 9 7 5 3

To Francis Labutte, with thanks

Sylvia Plath was in Paris on her own. She had a hotel room on Rue de Lille, after finding many other hotels full; she'd arrived in the city at a busy time, the weekend before Easter. Hôtel de Béarn, in the Saint-Germain neighbourhood, was one street from the River Seine, and a short walk to the Pont Royal, one of the many bridges over the river.

Easter 1956 was her second visit to Paris. Her first had been three months earlier, over Christmas 1955, when she had been mostly in the company of Richard Sassoon, a boyfriend she had begun seeing at the end of 1954. Richard had grown up in France but he was studying at Yale when Sylvia met him. He went back to living in Paris, teaching; and then he won a place to study at the University of Paris, at the Sorbonne.

On Christmas morning, 1955, Sylvia and Richard went to Notre Dame. Just two years earlier, aside from one day at home, Sylvia had spent Christmas in a psychiatric hospital still recuperating from a breakdown and suicide attempt. In Paris, no doubt she felt things were good, with a man she described as 'brilliant, intuitive, and alive'.[1] The two sat together in the enormous interior of the cathedral, the darkness illuminated by the jewelled colours of the stained-glass windows.

The trip ended disastrously though. On the eve of her departure from Paris, Richard told Sylvia he wanted a separation and asked her not to contact him again. His story was that he was returning to America to set up a business and that would be his future focus. But there was also talk of him having a Swiss girlfriend, who was intent on marrying him. The end of that Christmas visit was the last time she'd seen Richard.

At the Hôtel de Béarn, a week before Easter, Ted Hughes was in her head. Four weeks earlier they had met for the first time at a boozy party in Cambridge. They'd also spent one night together: the night before she left England for Paris. But they had no dating history, no formal relationship, and hadn't even confirmed any future meet-ups, or plans. Sylvia had a sense that something had started between them, though, something possibly significant.

Ted was in her head, but the thing most on her mind on her journey to Paris for Easter was that it was a chance to rekindle her relationship with Richard, who was living close to her hotel. Sylvia's connection with Richard was at times electrifying. When she read D.H. Lawrence's story 'The Man Who Died', she reflected on Richard's role in her life, how through him she had discovered 'the flaming of life'.[2]

Theirs was a relationship which was a lot more physical and a lot less regimented than constricted, conventional middle-class dating in the America of the 1950s. Elinor Friedman Klein, one of Sylvia's friends at Smith College, later wrote: 'We were brought up to be good little girls and we wanted to make our parents proud of us. In those days "good" equalled "married".'[3]

Sylvia seemed to thrive off the drama of the relationship with Richard. They were both volatile, with shaky physical and mental health. Reading

---

[1] Peter K. Steinberg and Karen V. Kukil (eds.), *The Letters of Sylvia Plath, Volume 1: 1940–1956*, (HarperCollins, 2017), 1090

[2] Karen V. Kukil (ed.), *The Journals of Sylvia Plath 1950-1962*, (Faber and Faber, 2000) 229

[3] Andrew Wilson, *Mad Girl's Love Song* (Scribner, 2016), 331

Sylvia's letters to Richard, and her journals, it's hard to tell the pursuer from the pursued. She also wrote to her mother about him on many occasions, although Mrs Plath may not have welcomed the idea of Richard as suitable husband material on the basis of some of Sylvia's descriptions of him: a 'weird, serious little guy', for example. She told her that Richard's eyes were black and shadowed 'as if he were an absinthe addict'.[4]

Sylvia had completed a degree at Smith College in Massachusetts, and was in Cambridge on a Fulbright scholarship to study literature at the University. She was delighted to be in England, and, in her words, 'on the brink of the continent'.[5]

Before her first trip to Paris, in a letter to her mother, Sylvia said she yearned to see 'the blazing lights and wonders of [the] city'.[6] Paris, to Sylvia, was a mythical place which promised light and delight and deep experiences. Maybe we all have such places in our minds. Where we imagine uncaging ourselves and discovering the secrets of life.

When Sylvia Plath arrived in England at the end of September 1955, it was her first time in Europe. She had spent her life in Massachusetts. Her mother, Aurelia, was a second-generation American of Austrian descent, and her father, Otto, was from

Grabow in northern Germany (he'd arrived in the USA aged fifteen, in 1900).

Otto died in 1940; Sylvia had just turned eight. The experience of losing her father permeated so much of her life and work (especially her late poetry). Her mother loved and cared for her diligently, perhaps over-diligently; Sylvia felt both supported and suffocated. In the hundreds of letters Sylvia wrote to Mrs Plath, she tended to downplay her troubles, perhaps to avoid worrying her mother, but also to reassure her she was successfully making her way in the world. If she did let negativity or upset into her letters home, she would invariably apologise in a letter a day or two later.

During the summer of 1953, aged twenty, Sylvia worked as a guest editor at *Mademoiselle* magazine in New York. What happened that summer is familiar to readers of Sylvia Plath's auto-biographical novel *The Bell Jar*. She began writing *The Bell Jar* in 1961; the novel was published under a pseudonym shortly before her suicide in 1963.

She relished the opportunity at *Mademoiselle*,

---

[4] *Letters, 1*, 733
[5] Ibid., 1093
[6] Ibid., 1033

but a whirlwind social schedule in New York, the tensions in her own life, and a crushing series of events and encounters – including sexual assault – precipitated a breakdown. In August 1953, back home, Plath attempted suicide by swallowing sleeping pills and hiding herself away in a crawl space in the cellar. She was missing for two days until her brother Warren heard a faint moan and found her. Sylvia was hospitalised, and received treatment with electro-shock therapy.

By the time she arrived at Cambridge aged twenty-two, she was familiar with, and almost resigned to, the challenges of a life of depression. In a letter to Richard Sassoon, she told of her resolve to embrace moments of positivity: 'I feel now as if I were building a very delicate intricate bridge quietly in the night, across the dark from one grave to another while the giant is sleeping.'[7]

Writing had become a key to survival and a calling: 'I re-create the flux and smash of the world through the small ordered word patterns I make,' she declared.[8] By mid-1955, she had written several accomplished poems, including 'Mad Girl's Love Song', which she attempted to place at the *New Yorker*, and 'Circus in Three Rings', which was published in the *Atlantic Monthly*. Generally, at this point in her life, her poems were well-crafted, impersonal, reticent.

At the time she arrived in Cambridge, Sylvia and Richard were still a couple – although in the second half of 1955, her letters and journal entries mention various suitors, and several platonic and not-so-platonic male friends.

Mid-December, Sylvia was expressing a little disappointment with her first months in Europe. She had struggled to make female friends. Some of the dull English girls at Cambridge were jealous of her, or dismissive, or both. Novelist Antonia Byatt was at Cambridge at the time: 'she had bobby socks and totally artificial bright red lips […] She just seemed silly,' she told the *New York Times* in 1991.[9] Apparently, a young woman who wears bright red lipstick and dyes her hair blonde can't possibly be taken seriously as a person, let alone a poet.

Plath was aware of her own failings, and deeply felt the pressure to meet the standards expected of her, to be a good little girl. In the run-up to end-of-term and the Paris trip, she writes that the hardest thing she has to accept in life is 'not being

[7] Ibid., 1037
[8] *Journals*, 232
[9] *New York Times*, 26 May 1991

perfect'.[10] She sensed she needed a break, stimulation, something other than cold Cambridge: 'I do want: theater, light, color, paintings, wine and wonder.'[11]

+

Years before she arrived in the city, Sylvia Plath had imagined Paris. Paris had been the home of semi-permanent and long-stay American expatriates like Gertrude Stein and Ernest Hemingway. Sylvia revered James Joyce, who had settled in the city. She knew the work of the French Impressionists, and loved Debussy.

The lure of Paris for bookish American students was irresistible. One of Sylvia's favourite poets, T.S. Eliot – a young American, like Plath, awarded a scholarship to study in England – was enchanted by French writers, including Baudelaire, Verlaine, and Jules Laforgue. In 1910, aged twenty-two, he took a room near the Sorbonne (where he studied philosophy). Nearly fifty years later, he confessed: 'I had at that time the idea of giving up English and trying to settle down and scrape along in Paris and gradually write French.'[12]

A stay in Paris could be transformative, in so many ways. Audrey Hepburn in the 1954 film *Sabrina* goes to Paris in pigtails and polka dots to study at a cooking school, and returns to the States wearing a

Givenchy suit, and exuding mesmerising Parisian chic. A sense of chic is something Plath always appreciated.

In 1949, Jacqueline Bouvier – later John F. Kennedy's wife and First Lady of the United States – lived in Paris on a study-abroad programme run by Smith College. The Paris she, American students, and other white, educated visitors experienced was concentrated in just a few neighbourhoods on the Left Bank: Saint-Germain, and the Sorbonne and the Quartier Latin.

The particular attraction of the city went beyond enlightenment and romance: Paris was a city with a permissive reputation. The writer James Baldwin said that American expatriate students in Paris had an opportunity to 'embrace irresponsibility'.[13] Bouvier lost her virginity in a hotel elevator to a writer from the *Paris Review* magazine.

In the mid-1950s, Paris was home to James Baldwin, as it was to other African-American writers – including Richard Wright, Langston Hughes,

---

[10] *Letters, 1*, 1050

[11] Ibid., 1036

[12] T.S Eliot in an interview in the *Paris Review*, 21, 56

[13] James Baldwin, 'A Question of Identity', in *Notes of a Native Son* (Penguin, 2017), 129

and Chester Himes – and entertainers. Black jazz musicians had lit up Montmartre and Pigalle since the mid-1920s. For these writers and entertainers, Paris was both a refuge and a place that progressed their work.

Baldwin moved to Paris in November 1948. It was deeply uncomfortable – and dangerous – to be a black homosexual, even in relatively liberal New York. He'd grown up assaulted by prejudice and racism. He could feel the racism corroding his soul; he feared the hate that hate made.

Baldwin took a room close to Café de Flore in the heart of Saint-Germain. In the years after the liberation, Café de Flore had a reputation for attracting a left-wing, existentialist crowd. It was a place Baldwin liked to be, socialising and writing. When Sylvia Plath arrived in Paris just before Easter 1956, Baldwin was working on the final draft of *Giovanni's Room*, his magnificent novel set in 1950s Paris, the world he knew so well, of expatriates, gay bars, desire, faithlessness, and illicit liaisons.

During her visits to Paris, Sylvia Plath walked many of the same streets as James Baldwin; a chance meeting would have been something amazing but Baldwin's favourite gay bars weren't on Sylvia's nighttime itinerary. Sylvia and Richard left Montmartre way before the all-night jazz began at Baldwin's favourite venues (dancing wasn't really her thing, although she had learned to mambo at a series of dancing lessons her mother had paid for in the summer of 1955). Furthermore, the chances of Sylvia smoking hashish in one of his favourite Arab cafés were next to zero.

It's striking how relatively little of Paris most students and visitors experienced. If Sylvia had gone beyond bourgeois Paris, out to working-class neighbourhoods like Belleville and Ménilmontant, for example, she'd have found there so much less light, and a lot less wealth.

The Ménilmontant of 1955 and 1956 is memorably captured in a short film called *Le ballon rouge* made by Albert Lamorisse, and featuring his young son Pascal. Pascal finds a red balloon that has a life of its own and the boy and the balloon become friends. The balloon's bright colour and buoyant sense of fun and freedom are a striking contrast with the grey post-war streets of unlit and unliterary Paris.

Christmas with Richard met Sylvia's expectations of Paris, as she reported to her mother in a letter sent on the last Friday of December 1955: 'Oh, it is all so amazing here, and so lovely. I've seen all the tourists want to see and so much more, because

I've had room to live.'[14] Nothing was more wonderful than room to live; she underlined <u>live</u>.

On that first visit, Plath took a hotel in the Quartier Latin, on Rue de la Harpe, just two hundred and fifty metres from the Sorbonne. She had a blue velvet room overlooking a noisy street of foreign restaurants.

With Richard, Sylvia strolled along the Seine, frequently crossing on to the Île de la Cité – an island in the Seine where a number of major buildings are sited, including Sainte-Chapelle and the cathedral of Notre Dame. The Île de la Cité is described by novelist Émile Zola in *L'Œuvre* as 'riding forever at anchor in the Seine, cradling the heart of Paris through which its blood has pulsed for centuries'.[15] In the novel, the lovers Claude and Christine are drawn to the river; it seems to fuel their desire. A river is a life force, primal, powerful, but always, of course, with the potential to be destructive too. In a defining incident in another Zola novel, *Thérèse Raquin*, a man is drowned in the Seine by his wife's lover.

On both her Christmas and Easter vacations, Plath often retraced her steps, visiting and revisiting her favourite places, and pausing on the bridges to watch the river flow. One of her most-walked routes was over the river, then through the Jardin des

Tuileries to Rue Scribe where the American Express office cashed cheques, and received wired funds. Travelling American tourists in a city routinely gave c/o American Express as an address where letters could be sent. Sylvia had invited people to write to her there during Christmas vacation, and again at Easter.

Once during her Christmas trip, Sylvia and Richard spent all afternoon in the Jardin des Tuileries. She liked to sketch there while sitting on one of the metallic chairs in the park, and was a regular at a green citronade *kiosque* in the gardens. It was a peaceful place; geometrical, gravel pathways between lines of trees, and some carefully arranged 18th- and 19th-century sculptures. At either end, the art galleries, the Louvre and the Orangerie. But also very close to the Seine.

She was at ease in the Tuileries; perhaps the gardens matched the sensibility of her poems up to late 1955, which were much more decorative than those of her later years. The gardens are situated between the lawless unconscious turbulence of the river and the famous galleries of studiously created framed art. She'd found a controlled space, some order, watching

---

[14] *Letters, 1*, 1069
[15] Émile Zola, *L'Œuvre* (OUP, 2008), 207

the world go by, with a lemonade and a sketch book.

+

Over the Christmas vacation in 1955, Sylvia and Richard had enjoyed ten days together, including a short train trip out of Paris, down to the warmer air of the south of France. But when Richard said he wanted the relationship to end, she gathered that, in her words, he wanted severance: 'a break clean and scrupulous as the edge of a guillotine'.[16]

Back in Cambridge in January 1956, Sylvia sent a series of upbeat letters home to her mother which gave no hint of the problems with her relationship with Richard. Soon, though, Sylvia was writing one of her least positive letters to Mrs Plath, admitting she was discouraged and desperate. Her fears seemed mostly to do with her desire, her need, to write. One of her strategies for building a delicate bridge through life was to write her way out of despair. But she was blocked, alone, mute.

Even though Richard wanted a clean break, and asked her not to contact him, still she wrote him letters. She also wrote to her mother that she'd been thinking about the possibility of having children with Richard but was concerned about his fluctuating health. It's not clear she was seriously considering this, or whether, under pressure from Mrs Plath, she felt the need to provide some kind of vaguely promising update on her marriage and baby prospects.

Her mood was prone to oscillate between giddy optimism and bleak despair. She could make confident plans and pronouncements, but within a day or two it was all dark again. Holding things together was a challenge. A heavy cold could trigger negativity, the disappointment of a story being rejected by the *New Yorker* could send her crashing.

Near the end of February 1956, fearing she was descending into a deeper depression, Sylvia paid a visit to the university psychiatrist. Calmed, she began to plan for a party she was heading off to in the evening. A party for the arty poetry crowd.

Ted Hughes was regularly staying in Cambridge even though he had graduated from there and had been doing various jobs in London – including a zoo attendant, and script reader for J. Arthur Rank film studios. That Saturday evening, he was in the company of a girl called Shirley who he'd been seeing for several months. Like Sylvia, they were attending the launch party of *St Botolph's Review*, a

---

[16] *Journals*, 218

new poetry magazine which included four poems by Hughes.

Sylvia had some sherry alone in her room, got ready to go out, accessorised with silver earrings, a red headband, and red shoes. Her date for the night was Hamish Stewart. They had so many whiskies in Miller's Bar before the party that Sylvia became unsteady on her feet. A jazz combo played in one room. She managed several conversations with various poets before encountering Ted Hughes. They detached themselves from Shirley, Hamish, and the crowd, shared some brandy and exchanged a fierce, feral kiss. In her journal the next day she reported that after he'd kissed her on the neck, she bit him hard on the cheek. Blood ran down his face. 'I screamed in myself, thinking: oh, to give myself crashing, fighting, to you.'[17]

Hamish described the party-goers as 'phonies' and told Sylvia that Hughes was 'the biggest seducer in Cambridge'.[18] Eventually they went back to Hamish's room, made love, and then, around 2.30 a.m., walked back to Sylvia's lodgings (there were strict university regulations forbidding overnight stays).

In the aftermath of what she called a 'sluttish night',[19] she wrote almost deliriously about Hughes, but prepared herself to be disappointed: 'I shall never see him again'.[20] (It turned out to be Hamish who disappeared from her life.) In a flurry of energy she poured her thoughts into several poems. One poem, begun the day after the party, is 'Pursuit'. In her journal, Plath describes 'Pursuit' as a poem about 'the dark forces of lust'.[21]

She'd been reading Baudelaire's poetry, and absorbed his vision of lust as an overriding sensation that stripped away decorum, and had the potential to spark transcendence, but, equally, catastrophe. She found something transfixing about Baudelaire's depictions of animal, dangerous lust. For one thing, it chimed with something she'd written five years earlier: 'I desire the things that will destroy me in the end.'[22]

Her journal entries could be studied and sculpted, but at other times feverish. After first meeting Ted she wrote, 'I am so hungry for a big smashing creative burgeoning burdened love',[23] and

---

[17] Ibid., 212
[18] Ibid., 213
[19] Ibid.
[20] Ibid., 212
[21] Ibid., 214
[22] Ibid., 55
[23] Ibid., 233

dubbed Ted a 'marauder'.[24] Processed in her mind, a brief moment with Hughes had been magnified through her theories, reading, and deepest fantasies. Hughes had become the dangerous lover, the force, the thrill, and the threat.

At her lowest moments, she confesses a desperation to fill the void created by the loss of her father. 'I cry so to be held by a man; some man, who is a father.'[25] Can one man fulfil the role of marauder and father? A protector and a danger?

Even after that first encounter with Ted at the end of February had made such an impact on her, Sylvia continued to send Richard letters. Early in March she wrote, 'The essential tragic fact; I love you with all my heart and soul and body.' She was frustrated by his intransigence, telling him, 'I see not why I should not live in Paris with you.'[26]

The last she'd heard, Richard had told her he was going to be in Spain for the whole time she was planning to be in Paris, but Sylvia found this hard to believe. Her writing was going well, though; this always made her happy. 'Fortunately, today, I could write ten novels and vanquish the gods,' she wrote on 9 March.[27]

Sylvia was dating a Fulbright student from Yale called Gary Haupt. Although they had a lot of interests in common, things soon cooled between them. Gary, however, was planning to travel with friends to Paris over Easter too, and Sylvia and he agreed to meet while they were both there. She realised she might like escorts, dates, and friendly faces in Paris if Richard turned out not to be in the city; for example, she had a note of the hotel address of a friend of a friend called Tony Gray, who was in Paris with his sister.

Sylvia's Easter vacation plan was to be in Paris for thirteen days, then, on Friday, 6 April, to meet an ex-boyfriend from back home, Gordon Lameyer. The plan was to go to Venice and Rome with Gordon. They'd dated for two years, from February 1953 onwards. She writes of his 'solidity'.[28] His support during her breakdown was appreciated (he is the model for Buddy Willard in *The Bell Jar*). Their relationship was still companionable enough to contemplate vacationing together.

Four weeks after the boozy Cambridge party, and the day before she was taking the ferry

---

[24] Ibid.

[25] Ibid., 199

[26] *Letters, 1*, 1128

[27] Ibid., 232

[28] *Journals*, 566

over to France, Sylvia started her journey to Paris by making her way from Cambridge to London. She'd been invited to break her journey in London by Luke Myers; he and Ted were staying there, on Rugby Street near the British Museum, in a flat owned by a friend's father. The flat was in a grungy, four-floor multi-occupancy house, with one shared unlit and unlovely lavatory in the basement.

She stayed over with Ted at this second encounter, the day before Paris. The sex with Hughes was so rough that arriving in her room at the Hôtel de Béarn, she reports washing and seeing in the mirror her face 'battered [...], smeared with a purple bruise from Ted and my neck raw and wounded, too'. Then, in a curious phrase, which – given what we know of her life and poetry – would take several decades of psychiatric training to unpick, she describes 'a sleepless holocaust night with Ted'.[29]

She'd woken up in the shared house in Rugby Street; by twilight, Sylvia was in Paris, excited, and too hungry and impatient to sleep. Once washed, she resolved to go find the small *pension* at 4 Rue Duvivier where Richard was staying. However, she realised she'd lost her map of Paris during her journey over.

Setting off, she encountered an Italian man who had been using the telephone in the lobby of the hotel, and he offered to loan her his street map. Plath had no knowledge of Italian, and Giovanni knew no English, so they talked French (his was good, hers was enthusiastic but basic). She explained a little about herself and Giovanni invited her to walk along Boulevard Saint-Germain and have dinner with him. They shared steak tartare and wine and meringue. Sylvia discovered he was Paris correspondent for the *Paese Sera* newspaper, a Communist journal based in Rome.

Back at the hotel, having diverted from her mission to find Richard, she slept on her own. The next day, Palm Sunday, her first full day in Paris, she left the hotel and walked through Saint-Germain along Rue Saint-Dominique, and on to Rue Duvivier. For weeks she'd been imagining herself in Paris calmly, quietly confronting Richard. She was confident of a result: 'My will and my love can melt doors.'[30] But it was not to be; when Sylvia arrived at Richard's place, the concierge confirmed he had indeed gone to Spain.

Sylvia asked the concierge for some paper so she could write a note to Richard. She cried and wrote; she wrote and wrote. On the radio Nat King

---

[29] Ibid., 552
[30] Ibid., 217

Cole was singing, '*Smile though your heart is aching*'. She couldn't smile; her tears fell on the paper as she wrote to Richard. So, after all, it was over, and she'd be in Paris without him. He had left no forwarding address, and to compound her distress her letters begging him to return early from Spain to meet her were on the concierge's desk, unopened, unread.

+

The concierge at 4 Rue Duvivier had a black poodle which nuzzled at Sylvia's leg as she wrote her distressed notes to Richard. Maybe it seemed to her that the dog was the only living creature that cared about her pain, but it was enough. Sylvia dried her tears, patted the poodle, and took a wander through the fruit stalls at the Champ de Mars, an open green space overlooked by the Eiffel Tower.

At a café close by, Sylvia ordered a plate of cold meats, and a coffee, which was served in the traditional style, short and black, but Sylvia didn't like the bitter taste and ordered a coffee with milk. As she drank and ate she read Jean Anouilh's play *Antigone* – one of her holiday reads – perhaps discovering these sentences that the young female protagonist says to King Creon: 'I will not be moderate. I will not be satisfied with the bit of cake you offer me if I promise to be a good little girl.' Antigone tells him she wants everything in life, immediately ('*Moi, je veux tout, tout de suite, et que ce soit entier*').

The second coffee was more to her taste; she was thrilled by *Antigone*. 'I felt downright happy,' she wrote in her journal. She describes how a calmness came over her that Sunday morning, an awakening. It's a beautiful moment, Plath's realisation of liberation and belonging: 'I had as much right to take my time eating, to look around; to wander & sit in the sun in Paris as anyone'.[31]

Sylvia walked along the Seine browsing the offerings of the book stalls along the Left Bank and crossed over to the Île de la Cité. She sat in the sun in the small park on the western tip of the island and began to sketch the Pont Neuf. It was a feature of her stay; at ease, content, she would draw. Over the next days she sketched bridges, a poster-covered advertising *kiosque*, a cat, and more besides. Her exuberance channelled inspiration from the environment. Crossing the bridges, the Paris sky opens up, the narrow streets of Saint-Germain emerge into the big horizons of what Plath called the 'gracious, spacious city'.[32]

---

[31] Ibid., 554
[32] Ibid., 346

Later that Palm Sunday, she met with Giovanni again. They took a ten-minute bus ride, beyond Bastille for dinner at Place Voltaire. She had two classic salads – *salades de tomates* and *celeriac remoulade* – and sardines, and then a pear for dessert. In a feverish sleep that night, Sylvia's memories of the night with Ted in London filled her mind, and worries that word might get back to Cambridge and reach censorious or gossipy ears.

On Monday, she moved rooms at the Hôtel de Béarn. She had spent some time that day looking for cheaper places, but the management at the Béarn offered her a smaller, attic room, saving her 30 francs a night, so she moved upstairs. The Béarn were providing her with breakfast croissants.

Just twenty-four hours after the disappointment and tears at Richard's absence, her outlook on her first Monday was very positive. The weather helped: it was sunny, the expansive Paris sky gloriously blue. She enthused to her mother about her room: 'the loveliest garret in Paris, overlooking the rooftops and gables'.[33]

During her walk to the American Express office at l'Opéra, just as she was at the river, a man started walking alongside her, trying to catch her eye. '*Charmante*,' he kept saying. Sylvia tried to play it cold – her usual response to street hassle – but she burst out laughing. They began to talk. He said he was Greek, said his name was Dimitri. She allowed him to draw a quick sketch in her notebook and they paused by the river. She began to distrust him, however, as he spun various stories about his wife being killed in the war, and eventually she managed to rid herself of him. At American Express she was told there were no letters for her. Instead of walking back to her hotel, Sylvia walked along the river to Boulevard Diderot to leave a note at Tony Gray's hotel; not having Richard Sassoon in Paris gave her the time and inclination to meet with other possibly like-minded people.

Later, in her journal, she considered her encounter with Dimitri and how she thought afterwards maybe she should have had sex with him. Spontaneity, accepting the moment, being a bit more Baudelaire: these were persistent themes in her journals. She dismissed the thought, though, acknowledging 'the danger is that this can turn to mere hedonism and escape to blindness and irresponsibility'. She wasn't going to 'embrace irresponsibility'[34] in the way Baldwin had described,

[33] *Letters, 1*, 1154
[34] *Journals*, 556

although the desire to do so didn't depart. As we shall see.

After a late afternoon siesta, Sylvia was woken by knocking on her door. It was Tony and his sister Sally. They had come to find her and take her for dinner. Sylvia thought Sally dour – she didn't drink wine. Sally made a remark about Sylvia's footwear (paper-thin red ballerina pumps). 'I could never wear shoes like yours,' Sally told her.[35]

Sylvia found Tony a little posh and tedious but wrote in her journal that having some human company was fun. They met again the next day, visiting the Eiffel Tower and having lunch together. Ironically, and to Sylvia's quiet delight, Sally's shoes were hurting her feet, and instead of a walk from the Tuileries to the Eiffel Tower, the three of them had to take a taxi.

At lunch, Sylvia ordered as cheaply as she could (cold chicken with salad, water, coffee); her spends for the day had gone on a ticket for that evening's performance of a play, *Ornifle* by Jean Anouilh, at the Comédie des Champs-Élysées. After the chicken salad, she took a walk, window-shopping along Rue Royale towards l'Église de la Madeleine, thrilled by shoes, furs and other delights along Rue Saint-Honoré and Rue de la Paix.

As her theatre visit neared, she decided to dress for the occasion, and wore a black velvet dress, and a mackintosh she described as having a 'swaggery cut', which she said made her feel 'chic'.[36]

There was an underlying reason why Sylvia stuck to her regular routes and to busy tourist areas; it was to do with personal safety. She began to dislike going out at dusk or after dark without a male escort, even when walking on familiar streets. She was aware, and wary, of running 'the gauntlet of the Paris streets at night where men are always at your elbow'.[37]

That evening, walking to the theatre, she crossed the river and walked along the Right Bank towards Place de la Concorde and then she realised she was being followed by a car. The driver, after following her, drove round the block and began following her again, then got out of the car and tried to speak to her. Sylvia walked faster, telling him she was going to the theatre, and managed to get rid of him. The trip to the theatre was not as enjoyable as she had hoped, partly because she was still spooked by the unwanted attention she'd got on her way to the play.

---

[35] Ibid.

[36] Ibid., 558

[37] Ibid., 557

The following day, Gary Haupt appeared while she was sketching a poster-stand near the Louvre. It was a welcome encounter; she says in her journal she was very pleased to see a friendly face. He introduced her to some friends of his and they went to a bar for a cognac.

Although their love affair was over, Sylvia and Gary enjoyed a couple of days together. One day they sat on a bench by the Palais de Justice and sketched a *tabac* and a café opposite. Gary also joined her on her daily walk to American Express where, once again, no letters were waiting for her. Then they went to the nearby Pam Pam for lunch.

That afternoon, back in the Tuileries, a gypsy woman sold Sylvia a helium-filled blue balloon on a long string with little tricolour streamers attached. As they walked through the park and then along the Seine, the balloon bobbed overhead, catching the attention of children who reached up wide-eyed and shouted '*Ballon!*'

In *Le ballon rouge*, the red balloon becomes a symbol of joy and life. Unknowingly, that afternoon, it was as if she was enacting a version of the film; Sylvia lapped up the fun and excited attention from the kids, describing herself as being 'elated' all afternoon.

Sylvia and Gary spent an evening at Sérail on

Rue de la Harpe in the Quartier Latin, a little walk from her hotel. Sérail was somewhere she knew; she'd eaten there in December with Richard. Perhaps inevitably, the return brought back memories, the blue velvet bedroom at her Christmas vacation hotel was the same shade of blue as the balloon she'd bought, she realised. Her mood was a little deflated as she parted from Gary and went back alone to her hotel.

Another day that week, Gary organised a lovely evening for them in Montparnasse, beginning with a meal at Brasserie Lutetia on Boulevard Raspail and then on to a cinema, the Studio Parnasse on Rue Jules Chaplain, where they saw *Dreams That Money Can Buy*, an experimental film made by the artist Hans Richter in Manhattan in 1947, and featuring a series of surreal dream sequences created by the likes of Max Ernst, Marcel Duchamp, and Man Ray. Words at the beginning of the film declare that everybody dreams, and everybody travels; sometimes to countries where 'strange beauty, wisdom, adventure [and] love' await. This, says the narrator, 'is a story of dreams mixed with reality'.

+

Good Friday, 30 March, was perhaps the strangest day of Sylvia Plath's stay, passing through bliss, abandon, confusion, and self-questioning. In the morning, she crossed Pont Royal and met Tony, whose sister had returned home. They had a lemonade together in Sylvia's favourite *kiosque* in the Tuileries, and then set off for Montmartre by métro, revisiting many of the places she'd been to with Richard at Christmas, including Sacré-Cœur. Sylvia had her portrait rendered by a silhouette cutter, and they lunched just off the Place du Tertre. The restaurant – the Auberge du Coucou – later came under new ownership and was renamed Chez Plumeau; it remains on the site to this day.

In her journals, Sylvia described what they ordered for lunch, including a 'miraculous' veal sautéed in mushrooms, and a bottle of white wine. After her return from Paris, the Cambridge student paper *Varsity* published a double-page article by Plath entitled 'April in Paris'. The style she adopted was breathless travelogue. She describes how the wine and food 'sent us floating into the afternoon like larks', which is certainly one way of describing their afternoon.

The wine and food had softened their mood. Tony was being attentive, even intimate – he put his arm around her and bought her flowers. 'I mellowed to [his] fondness […] in the pale gold aura of wine,' she wrote, 'and felt most beautiful and slightly damned'.[38]

Tony pointed out they could get on the métro at Rue des Abbesses (a short walk down the hill from the restaurant) and that would take them direct to the station halfway along Rue du Bac, just two hundred metres from Sylvia's hotel. So they took *ligne* 12 back to Saint-Germain.

There were no signs of saying goodbye. Instead the two went to her hotel. They kissed and undressed. In the moments after they got naked, Sylvia went to the bathroom but when she returned Tony was getting dressed again. He'd had second thoughts about making love. She tried to work out what had happened; she decided he was sweet and dear, although a bit conceited, and too caught up in appearances and decorum.

A day or two later, she made notes to herself, lists of commandments.[39] She resolved to write more, to be 'chaste & subdued' the next term, and perhaps to take on the persona of a 'mystery woman'. Mystique, she realised, was a quality worth cultivating.

A few days from leaving Paris and still American

---

[38] Ibid., 562
[39] Ibid., 569

Express had no letters for her. On 2 April, making her daily trip there, she discovered that all her post had been forwarded on to England; at the end of her visit to Paris in December she'd asked them to send on any further mail to her address in Cambridge. They'd scrupulously been observing this request, even while she was making her Easter visit.

On her last full day in Paris, the sunny weather over, Sylvia spends the morning lying on her bright yellow bed quiet and warm as the rain falls on the streets and rooftops outside. She thinks and writes about Richard's absence, and fate; about accident and chance; about the 'foolish mistake' at American Express which severed her connections, not just from her mother, but from others too.

That's it though. Fate, decisions, a conversation with a stranger, a moment of irresponsibility, someone hearing your faint cry. And opportunities, choices, decisions. Richard, Ted: do the missing letters hold any clues? What's being said? What decisions have been made? Questions were falling like rain on the Paris rooftops.

Her last evening in Paris was spent with Giovanni, just as her first had been that Saturday night she'd arrived without a map, and again the Sunday when he helped to sustain her brightened mood after

she'd shed many tears over Richard. They'd dis-
cussed the art of Giorgio de Chirico, de Staël, and
the poetry of T.S. Eliot. She mentioned him in one of
her letters to her mother, declaring 'He is without a
doubt the nicest communist I've ever met'.[40] Plath
says in her journal, 'I considered sleeping with him',
but she is thankful afterwards that she didn't, partly
because of all the complications that could arise,
especially given that he had a wife in Italia and a
mistress in Paris.[41] Maybe the reality of having sex
with Giovanni wasn't important; the knowledge it
was an option was enough.

It appears that she talked about her love life
to Giovanni, describing to him how, in her words, 'the
alternatives revolve in a fatal dance'.[42] In her journal
she was admitting Richard's 'dark image still haunts
me'.[43] Even on her last day in Paris, she was wondering
if Richard would appear back in the city and try to
find her, and Plath acknowledged that if he did, she
would go to him. But it was not meant to be; even
though on her return to Cambridge she'd discovered

---

[40] *Letters, 1*, 1155
[41] *Journals*, 565
[42] Ibid., 567
[43] Ibid., 566

some letters he'd sent to her, he'd not been there for her in Paris.

No doubt she also tried to explain to Giovanni about her relationship with Gordon, her ex-boyfriend she was about to vacation with. It seems, though, that solid, dependable Gordon was never going to be unorthodox or dangerous enough to be attractive to Sylvia.

During the time Gordon and Sylvia had in Paris together, he took her photograph outside Notre Dame, then they travelled by train to Munich, where they broke their journey to Italy, taking separate hotel rooms near the station. They stopped in Venice for two days, then on 9 April moved on to Rome. Most of her sightseeing Sylvia chose to do alone, as her relationship with Gordon had become fraught and argumentative.

One day at the American Express in Rome, Sylvia received a letter from Ted arranging for her to go back to Rugby Street on the night of her return to England. Once she'd returned to Cambridge, she would also find a letter from Ted which had been forwarded from the Paris American Express office. In the latter – it was just five sentences and a PS – he noted his delight at discovering the smoothness of her skin at their first Rugby Street night. The PS was a request to bring back two bottles of brandy.

Few of Sylvia's boyfriends and other male friends have talked about their relationship with her; Giovanni Perego has remained silent, and Richard Sassoon has said little apart from confessing he's lost most of her letters to him. Gordon has been more forthcoming. He described their last breakfast together in Rome; Sylvia got up brusquely from the breakfast table, and walking out of the hotel's dining room, crashed into a transparent glass door.

It was Friday, 13 April, her father's birthday, and Sylvia had a rendezvous with Ted, again at the Rugby Street flat; he said he would be expecting her after 8 p.m. It had been exactly three weeks since they had last seen each other. Sylvia returned to England from Rome on a mist-shrouded flight, with some things clearer in her mind. In a letter to her mother, she wrote that by the time she'd read Richard's letters, it was 'too late, after feeling terribly deserted in Paris'.[44] She arrived back in England, drew a line under what she now called her 'old life', and decided to pledge herself, solely, completely, to Ted.[45]

In one of her later poems, 'Lady Lazarus',

---

[44] *Letters, 1*, 1160
[45] *Journals*, 336

written in October 1962, Plath alludes to both the
biblical character Lazarus who was brought back to
life by Jesus and the mythical bird, the phoenix. Her
fascination with Lazarus dated back to the aftermath of
being discovered by Warren after her suicide attempt,
and a sense of returning from the dead. Paris seems
to have been a time of self-discovery, and a chance
for Plath to shape a new life. It was appropriate that
she was there at Easter, a time of death, resurrection,
renewed hope.

A day or two after her latest night with Ted
in Rugby Street, and back in Cambridge, she wrote to
Richard, telling him of something that had started
two months ago (she is referring to meeting Ted
Hughes at the literary party). 'It needed not to have
happened,' she says, 'just as it needed not to have
happened that you wrote that you did not want to
see me in Paris'.[46] She writes that a choice has to be
made, and that back in England there was now 'only
one way of happening'. Her words are opaque, and
far from direct, but it was her way of communicating
to him that it was over, she had embarked on a new
relationship. Perhaps she was choosing to be opaque
to torture him with uncertainty and leave the details
to his imagination.

That first week back from Paris saw Ted follow

her to Cambridge and the reunited pair in each
other's company almost non-stop, and also a surge
in Sylvia's writing output, including a poem called
'Ode to Ted', a portrait of a powerful, even enslaving,
colossus, a man in control of his environment.
There's a playfulness in the poem which undercuts
some of the threat emanating from the subject's
intimidating presence, but it's clear that Sylvia did
not see Ted as the safest choice. In a long letter to
her mother during that week, there's no illusion, no
candy-coated romance. Ted is 'brilliant […] a world-
wanderer and vagabond,' she writes. 'I am terrified
even to have known him, he makes all others mere
puny fragments. Such a torment & pain to love him.'[47]

Ted left London in May and moved to
Cambridge, where he lived with Luke Myers in
Tenison Road. He and Sylvia met every day, and their
relationship deepened into an irresistible obsess-
ion and connection. Not the least significant aspect
to the couple's life together was their fruitful, fertile
poetry partnership. Over the next years, the work
of both poets would improve almost beyond recogni-

---

[46] *Letters, 1*, 1164
[47] Ibid., 1161

tion from the inspiration and support they offered
each other. As early as 29 April 1956, Sylvia is full of
plans and confidence: 'within a year I shall publish a
book of 33 poems which will hit the critics violently
in some way or another. My voice is taking shape,
coming strong.'[48] By the end of the year she will have
completed several of the poems that will fill her first
collection, and 'November Graveyard', inspired by
the graveyard at St Thomas's church in Heptonstall,
close to the Hughes family home.

Sylvia Plath and Ted Hughes married on 16
June 1956 at the Church of St George the Martyr,
Queen Square, London. Sylvia's mother was a witness;
she'd arranged to be in Europe on vacation. On 21
June, Sylvia and Ted and Mrs Plath flew to Paris from
London, for a few days' sightseeing before Mrs Plath
left the couple. Sylvia and Ted stayed on for several
more days, then took the long train journey to Madrid.
Their honeymoon destination was Benidorm, where
they spent more than a month under blue skies (in
1981, Hughes helpfully explained their honeymoon
choice; Benidorm 'at that time still undeveloped
as a tourist resort'[49]). The couple enjoyed their stay;
Sylvia loved to walk round the markets and sit by the
harbour.

On 23 August, they returned to Paris, taking

a room at the Hôtel des Deux Continents in the heart of Saint-Germain. Their first morning, they went shopping for fruit. Sylvia took Ted to the stalls at Rue de Buci to buy a kilo of ripe red peaches. The stallholder moaned that everyone was asking for red peaches, and filled a bag with unripe green ones instead. While his back was turned, Sylvia took a rock-hard green peach out of the bag and replaced it with a red one. The man snatched back the bag and refused to serve them, raging *on n'a pas le droit de choisir* – one is not allowed to choose.

She wanted the ones she couldn't have, so she moved on, bought some red peaches from round the corner, and added some yellow pears to her shopping, before going on to their hotel. There, Sylvia took in the view, the grey light, the Paris roofs. 'I really love this city above any I've ever been,' she wrote to her mother.[50] Sylvia also expressed the hope that some day she and Ted would live together in Paris for a year.

It's not how the story will unfold. The couple will go to back to England, and visit the Hughes family in Yorkshire. She'll take advantage of a second

---

[48] Ibid., 1181

[49] Sylvia Plath, *Collected Poems* (Faber and Faber, 1981), 275

[50] *Letters, 1*, 1240

year on a Fulbright scholarship and they'll make their first home together in Cambridge.

Sylvia began helping Hughes get more of his poetry published. Her advocacy of his work included contacting an ex-boyfriend called Peter Davison who had just taken an influential job at the *Atlantic Monthly* in Boston. She sends him letters reviewing the tumultuous year since they'd last seen each other – not least her marriage to Ted Hughes – and tells him of her time in Europe and her travels. Paris is 'my second home', she says.[51]

The couple never returned to Paris. In April 1960, their daughter Frieda was born, and Nicholas in January 1962. In July 1962, Sylvia became aware that Ted was having an affair with Assia Wevill. On 30 July 1962, Sylvia sent a long letter to her psychiatrist back in the States, Dr Ruth Beuscher – Dr Nolan in *The Bell Jar* – telling her Ted is 'on the rampage', as if he's in thrall to the idea of destruction, in poetry and in life. She describes one of his recent poems, about a hawk, as 'pure ego-Fascist' and quotes the opening line ('I kill where I please because it is all mine'). She knows he knows she might kill herself 'over this'. 'This' is the 'other woman business'.[52]

In the letter she describes some physical symptoms of her trauma – nausea, shortness of breath – a trauma she characterises as a 'second loss of a second father'. But, she says, 'I want Ted to understand I am not a doll-wife who can be lied to & kept happy'.[53]

In September 1962, the couple will separate. She has with her the children, the youngest just a few months old. Her last poems – which, after her death, will be collected into a volume called *Ariel* – are crafted word patterns still but have evolved, and intensely alive now with conspicuous, harrowing emotion.

On 11 February 1963, in the midst of a freezing winter, Sylvia Plath ended her life; she is buried in the graveyard at St Thomas's, Heptonstall. Her mother will live until 1994. Giovanni Perego will remain elusive, Richard Sassoon will stay silent. Sylvia Plath never bumped into James Baldwin on the street, but they met after all, in the pages of the influential magazine *Critical Quarterly* in the summer of 1964. 'Two literary events of great importance have recently occurred,' announces the magazine's editor, A.E. Dyson. They are, he writes, the emergence of

[51] Ibid., 1252

[52] Peter K. Steinberg and Karen V. Kukil (eds.), *The Letters of Sylvia Plath, Volume 2: 1956–1963* (HarperCollins, 2018), 803

[53] Ibid., 804

James Baldwin as a 'powerful and original writer', and the publication of Sylvia Plath's later poems. The two writers had originated a new era of literature, painfully challenging what the magazine calls 'the tranquillized Fifties'.[54]

Sylvia had recognised that her writing helped build a delicate bridge to assist her in negotiating her way through life. During her last year, her poems were tracking its collapse, as the pain and emotion comes crashing, smashing through, like a river flooding ornamental gardens, the Seine demolishing the Tuileries.

+

Ted Hughes published a poem entitled 'Your Paris' in 1998, many years after Sylvia Plath's death, in a volume of poetry, *Birthday Letters*, articulating his thoughts and grief about Plath. In the interim he'd been overseeing her poetry collections, reading her journals, and writing the preface to various Plath publications, but he had rarely spoken about Sylvia and their relationship.

Hughes remained with Assia Wevill after Sylvia's death, although he had several affairs. In March 1969, she took her own life – and that of her daughter, Shura (Hughes never publicly acknowledged he was Shura's father).

Hughes became Poet Laureate in 1984, but there's a sense that his life after 1963 was in many ways defined by Plath. From the late 1970s especially, there was, and remains, a strong current flowing against him. At the time of writing, the word HUGHES is scratched out from the name SYLVIA PLATH HUGHES on Sylvia's grave. It's clear her death haunted, distracted and disrupted his life and work.

The 'Your Paris' poem is directly addressed to Sylvia, an exploration of their days and nights in Paris, staying at the Hôtel des Deux Continents. 'Your Paris, I thought, was American', says Hughes, which, the poem makes clear, is not just a statement of the obvious – his wife, after all, was American – it's a put-down.

He suggests she perceived a fantasy Paris. He lists the sources which had created her sense of the city, including writers in the interwar years like Hemingway, Fitzgerald, and Gertrude Stein. Her Paris, he suggests, was an aesthetic rather than realistic version.

Sylvia's excitement at stepping out of the hotel on to the street in a 'shatter of exclamations' – all her manic enthusiasm for the city – made Hughes

---

[54] *Critical Quarterly*, Summer 1964, 99

uncomfortable, he says in the poem, although he didn't take up these issues with her at the time. 'I wanted to humour you', he says.

He goes on to say, 'I kept my Paris from you.' His take is very different to hers. His perspective is of a city still recovering from Nazi occupation and collaboration. Where Sylvia relaxed into a chair outside a café that first morning and felt like she belonged, and lunched in Montmartre ordering tomato salad and veal and a golden white wine, Hughes saw bullet holes in buildings, sensed the ghosts of Nazi soldiers, and recrimination and reprisal in the waiters' eyes.

The poem sets up this contrast, not in the spirit of an interesting dialogue but as a judgement of her. And the implication is that while she is dazzled by the surface of things, the no-nonsense Yorkshireman has deeper, more authentic, insight. Hughes is not convinced by Plath's Paris: 'I was not much ravished by the view of the roofs.'

What's unnerving, is that there is no 'our', no shared vision, not even a shared bottle of wine; no sitting together on a café *terrasse* watching the world go by. The poem plays on the symbolism in the name of their hotel – Hôtel des Deux Continents – which functions as a way of suggesting that even at that point in the marriage Sylvia and Ted were as unconnected with each other as two continents. Touching from a distance.

In 'Your Paris', Hughes contends that Plath's bedazzlement by a surface, fantasy Paris is a reflection of something more ruinous: her resistance to confronting her pain, her despair. Plath was engaged in the world, full of life experience, well-read, and self-critical in a way that few of us could bear to be, but Hughes appears to be accusing her of hiding from her pain behind triviality. She was a 'walking wound' wrapped in 'gushy burblings', he says.

That someone so vulnerable could feel exuberant doesn't have to be a contradiction; it can be a fact. There is a difference between feeling pain, and successfully articulating it creatively as she did in later poems, like 'Daddy'. In 1956, she knew she was at the beginning of the process to find her voice as a poet, but is there evidence that Sylvia was unaware of her pain? Just a few moments scanning her journal entries would suggest otherwise. The line from her April 1962 poem 'Elm' speaks of a long-standing fear: 'I am terrified by this dark thing / that sleeps in me'.

Later in 'Your Paris', it appears there was something that had disturbed Hughes on a more personal level. Like the other poems in *Birthday Letters*, 'Your Paris' is written with the benefit of hindsight and the knowledge Hughes gleaned from reading Sylvia's journals and letters after her death. The poem appears to suggest Hughes's inability to enjoy Paris as she did was heightened by insecurity about Sylvia's relationship with Richard.

The past is not easy to shrug off. Being unsettled that someone who loves you has loved before is understandable perhaps. Not that no-nonsense Ted even comes close to admitting this, but reading of her relations with Giovanni, Tony, Gary, Gordon, perhaps even Dimitri, seems to have bruised him. Most of all, Richard, of course, to whom Sylvia pledged her love, time and again. The scene Sylvia describes in her journals – bereft at the concierge's desk at Richard's place – is directly referenced in the poem, Hughes recalling her letters waiting for him unopened.

At the close of the poem Hughes comes closest to tenderness, as he watches Sylvia drawing 'as by touch, / Roofs, a traffic bollard, a bottle, me.' The scene is loving, in one reading, maybe, but equally, perhaps, evidence that the deepest trauma for Ted Hughes is that Plath's suicide had occupied him, taken root in him, and his identity. Drawing him, she's capturing his likeness, and capturing him too; her life defined him, even, and especially, after her death. In contrast, Plath seems elusive to Hughes, not only because he couldn't share her enthusiasms, but couldn't pin her down. She has a life beyond him.

A week into her Easter visit, Sylvia reported how she had 'walked for miles and miles and seen much and wondered much'.[55] Compare her use of 'black shoe' in her poem 'Daddy' six years later – a constricting piece of footwear, a symbol of subjugation – to what she chose to wear in Paris: very lightweight, paper-thin red ballerina pumps. Walking, these gave her lightness, liberation, and a spring in her step.

She'd conquered loneliness and street hassle in Paris, to the point where she was able to express that she was 'proud [...] at my independence and courage'.[56] She'd discovered moments of happiness and inspiration, and retained a greater love for the city's intriguing, flawed charisma, its streets, the light, the wide horizons. Paris remained a special place of appeal and promise for Plath until her final months. At the end of 1962, Ted had agreed a separation settlement giving her £1000 cash. She reported that his relatives thought it possible she would take the money and flee to Paris with the children.[57]

One of my Parisian friends, Sixtine, once

---

[55] *Journals*, 560
[56] Ibid., 558
[57] *Letters, 2*, 847

explained why she liked one particular album by Serge Gainsbourg (*Histoire de Melody Nelson*).Within the music, Gainsbourg articulates all the female characteristics ('*les personnages féminins*') which she said she recognises in herself: '*Féminines, félines, fatales, enfantines, sensuelles, sexuelles, mystérieuses, joueuses, sauvages, séductrices, aimées, fragiles, fortes*'.

Ted Hughes's utilitarian perspective blocks him from being able to relate to Plath's joy, so he dismisses it. He looked at her joy and assumed she was delusional. He can't understand her without making her one-dimensional. He wants to understand her in order to define her. And to define in order to pin down and control the narrative. Of both their lives.

His perspective, and our perspective, is also coloured by the circumstances of Plath's death. He knows the end of the story, we know the end of the story; but the end of the story is not the whole story.

How could anyone question or begrudge her that exuberance? That moment she skipped through the streets feeling that she belonged. Her visits and revisits to her favourite places. Talking poetry and love and art and desire with Giovanni. Getting by on mangled French, paying extra for room-service croissants and café au lait every morning in her yellow-painted attic room. Looking chic on the sunny side of the street.

A brasserie on Boulevard Raspail, a surrealist film in Montparnasse. Hearing the Easter bells, crossing the river, the Seine flowing beneath her feet, the wide Paris sky arching towards all the horizons. She has as much right to those moments of happiness as any of us, perhaps more; her sketchbook in her hand, making her way to the park, in the sun, in her Paris.

ORIGINAL ILLUSTRATION, DESIGN & TYPESETTING
Zoë McLean, Manchester
zoe@confingopublishing.uk

BODY TYPE
Minion Pro, an updated and expanded version of
Robert Slimbach's early 90s design for Adobe.

COVER TYPE
Futura PT, developed at ParaType in 1995 by Vladimir
Yefimov, expands on the classic geometric sans-serif
typeface Futura designed by Paul Renner in 1927.

Searching For Love:
Courtney Love in Liverpool, 1982

'Meticulously researched, Haslam unpicks and unravels the barrage of
myths told about Love in Liverpool'
Anokhi Shah

'I loved every second of this read! A book littered with truth and
adventure at every turn'
Emma Aylett

CŌNFINGŌ

confingopublishing.uk